Together

Together
A Tale of Friendship

Daphne Deckers

Illustrated by Joey Holthaus

T tra.publishing

One fine morning,
Lev sat on the steps outside his door,
watching the sunrise.

Some days the sun came up from
the sea looking a little pale,

and others it stayed hidden
behind the clouds.

But today, the sunrise was spectacular.
It was so beautiful and fiery
that Lev forgot to eat his toast.

He wished he had someone
sitting beside him, who would say,
"Lev, will you look at that sunrise,
how beautiful, how fiery?"

And Lev would say,
"Yes, truly spectacular."

And they would both nod
their heads at the same time.

But watching
all that beauty by himself
made him wonder
if it really existed.

If you couldn't
share it with someone,
how could you know it wasn't
all just in your mind?

Two yellow butterflies fluttered
past in front of him. They were twirling
around each other, up and down.

"Good morning, butterflies," said Lev. "Have you seen how beautiful the sunrise is?"

But the butterflies didn't hear him.
They were too busy playing together.
They just kept on tumbling up
and tumbling down until they
disappeared from sight.

Lev wondered where you went when you disappeared. Would the yellow butterflies continue to flutter? Would they be wondering: Where is Lev? Is he still sitting on the steps?

Lev felt the weight of these questions
so early in the morning. Maybe it would
be better to just to watch the beautiful, fiery,
spectacular sunrise. And to eat his toast.

Lev got up and walked to the beach.

The sun shimmered on the water,
the waves lapped on the shore,
and a seagull circled in the sky.

As he sat in the sand,
the bird swooped
and landed by his feet.

"Good morning, seagull,"
Lev said. "Have you seen
the spectacular sunrise?"

He gestured towards the horizon,
but the seagull only had eyes
for the toast.

He snatched it
from Lev's hand.

He didn't get very far
before another seagull dove down
and made off with the toast.

The seagull looked crestfallen.

"You should have asked me," said Lev.
"I would have been happy to share it with you."

The seagull cocked his head
but said nothing.

Lev scratched behind his ear.

The birds, the butterflies–
they never said anything back.
Maybe they didn't understand him.

He often felt like
he was looking for something,
but he wasn't sure what.
He wanted to figure it out.

Lev got up and brushed the sand
off his clothes. He was about to head back
to his cottage when he saw an intriguing
dot on the tide line in the distance.
His eyes grew big.

A dot was mysterious and special.
As long as you didn't know what it was,
it could turn out to be anything.

The dot slowly grew larger
and Lev saw that it was a boy
with rolled up trousers,
walking barefoot through the surf.

"Hello!" waved Lev.
"Hello!"

Lev was so curious
about the unexpected visitor
that he walked towards him.

"I'm Lev," he said when he was
close enough to hold out his hand.
"And I'm Levi!" said the boy.

For a moment they stood facing
each other in silence, Lev and Levi.
There were so many questions. There were very
big questions, but also very small ones.
Which ones should they start with?

"Where are you from?"
asked Lev at last.

"I've come from
a faraway place,"
Levi said.

Wow, thought Lev,
someone who is
from far away.

Lev had never
traveled far himself.

He nodded towards the bag
Levi was carrying over his shoulder.
"Are you on your way somewhere?"

"I'm looking for friends," said Levi.
"But I'm not quite sure where to find them.
Can you help me?"

Lev wasn't sure how to answer that.
He didn't have friends, and he had
no idea where to find them.

"Well, I can offer you a drink,"
he said, pointing to his house.
"That would be nice," said Levi.

Once seated on the steps by the door,
each with a glass of lemonade,
Levi said that he had been planning
to take a different route.

"But then I suddenly spotted two yellow
butterflies tumbling around each other
so cheerfully and thought:
I wonder where they came from?
And I decided to find out."

"I saw those butterflies too," Lev said.
"I wondered where they were headed."
"To me," said Levi, "and I was headed to you."

Lev nodded,
thinking about the butterflies.
Maybe they understood
more than he had guessed.

Lev and Levi looked out towards the sea.
The sun was shining on the water,
but some grey clouds had come in as well.

"Shall I tell you
what I heard once?"
asked Lev.
"It's that you can
make friends."

"Make...?" said Levi
"But how?"

Lev bent down and
grabbed a fistful of sand.
"Maybe with this?" he wondered.
Levi looked at him, surprised.

"Why not?" said Lev.
"I've made big castles out
of sand before. And a whale.
And a dolphin.
So why not make a friend?"

Levi jumped up. "Let's try it!"

They ran to the beach together,
found the perfect spot, and started digging.

The seagull came to supervise
and cocked his head in wonder.

They started by making a big, round belly.
Lev fashioned arms
while Levi worked on the legs.

Last but not least, they made the head.
The head took them the longest because,
they agreed, the head of a friend
contains everything that really matters.

The sun slowly disappeared behind the clouds,
and the wind whipped up the waves,
but Lev and Levi did not even notice it.

They found two pretty shells
to give their sandy friend's eyes,
and finally Levi drew a big smile
on his face with his finger.
"He looks really cheerful," said Lev.
"It's a good start."

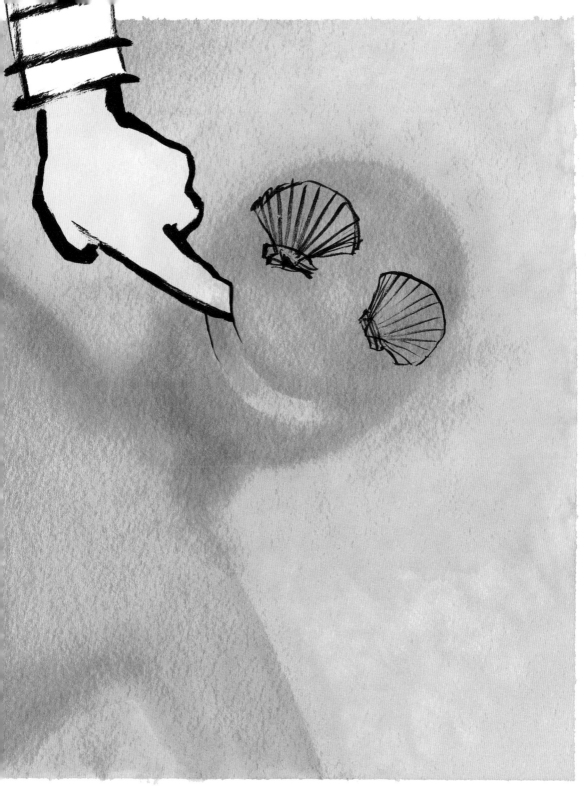

They admired their new friend from all
angles but didn't notice the big wave rolling
in from the sea. With a great big crash,
the wave washed over the sand.

Their sandy friend's arms and legs
were swept away, his tummy smooshed,
and when the water withdrew,
his smile had also disappeared.

"Oh dear,"
said Lev, "that wasn't
such a good start after all."
"Oh, but I think it was,"
said Levi, "because now
we know so much more
about making friends."

"What more do we know?"
asked Lev, who was glad
he no longer needed
to answer life's big questions
all by himself.

"Now we know that this wasn't
the friend we were looking for," said Levi.
"One wave, and he's gone. Let's make
a better one, one that won't wash away.
Let's build our new friend over there,
behind your cottage, on the edge of the forest."
Lev nodded.

"Ok, let's do it.
We'll make him
out of leaves!
He'll be
really soft."

"We can use lots
of different kinds of leaves,"
said Levi. "Red and brown leaves;
green and yellow ones, too.
That way our friend will be colorful." Lev
thought it was a great idea.

Isn't it wonderful, he thought,
that Levi comes from far away.
People from far away
seem to have exciting ideas.

They formed a head, two arms, and two legs out of the beautifully-colored leaves and kept the largest mound of them for the tummy. Laughing, Lev and Levi took turns tumbling into the soft leafy belly.

They had only just finished their
new friend when the sky turned dark.
The wind began to howl.

Trees rustled and sand whirled all
around them. The two boys covered
their eyes with their hands.

When they opened their eyes again,
their leafy friend had
been blown to pieces.

"What a pity," sighed Lev.
"He had such a nice, soft side to him."

Levi picked up a leaf from
the ground and thought long and hard.
"Maybe he was too soft,"
he said at last.

"Is there such a thing
as too soft?" asked Lev.
"Being soft is a good
thing, isn't it?"

"It's a great thing," Levi said,
"but you also need a little firmness,
so you won't be blown apart
by the first gust of wind."

Lev thought
about the yellow butterflies
who were dancing on the wind.

"Here's an idea," he said,
"let's make a friend out of branches.
Branches are firm,
but you can also bend them."

"What an excellent idea,"
Levi said.

They gathered straight branches
and crooked ones, large branches
and small ones, and braided them
all together into a firm friend who could
withstand wind or waves.

Levi wiped the sweat from his brow.
"We've been working on this friend
for a long time," he said, "but it feels
like time is passing quickly.
When I'm making something with you,
the clock seems to have a different rhythm."

Lev nodded.
He was going to say that he felt exactly the same.
That it was hard work, lugging all those
branches around, but that it also felt light
because he was sharing the load.

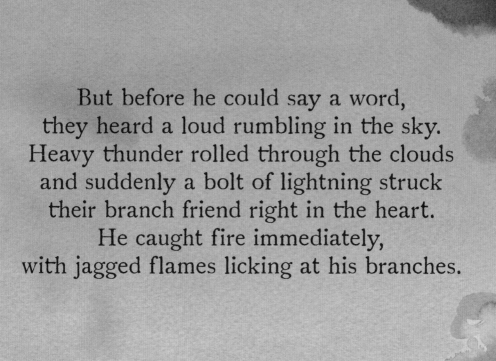

But before he could say a word,
they heard a loud rumbling in the sky.
Heavy thunder rolled through the clouds
and suddenly a bolt of lightning struck
their branch friend right in the heart.
He caught fire immediately,
with jagged flames licking at his branches.

Levi went very quiet.
But Lev knew exactly what to do:
"I've got sausages!
Why don't I go and get them?"
he smiled.

Lev and Levi sat together
beside the burning branches.
They had both threaded sausages onto sticks
and were roasting them over the fire.
"Mine is almost done," Lev said.
"That was lightning fast," Levi giggled.

After the thunderstorm, the air cleared.
The clouds drifted away,
and the sun came out again.

"We are learning more and more
about making friends," said Levi,
"but we clearly don't know everything
there is to know."

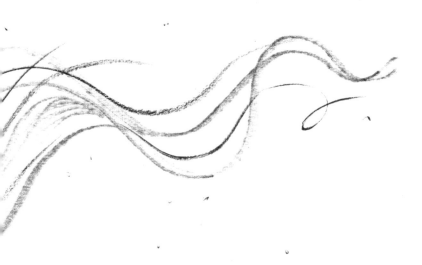

Lev took his sausage out of the fire.
"Do you think we will ever know
all there is to know?" he asked.
"Because that seems like a lot to me."

"Yeah, me too," said Levi.
"Maybe it happens bit by bit.
And after lots of bits, we will know everything."
Lev took a bite of his sausage
and pondered.

"I've got it," Lev said.

He pointed to the seagull, who was
sitting on a large rock smelling the sausages.
"Why don't we make a friend out of rocks.
Surely nothing could go wrong with that."

Levi clapped his hands in delight.
"That's it!
Come on, let's get started
straight away."

They spent the rest of the afternoon
collecting big and small rocks.
There was no need to move the biggest rock.
That would be the belly.
They rolled a head into place and made arms
and legs out of lots of different rocks.

"This one's a keeper," said Levi.
"He won't be washed away, he won't be
blown away, and he can't go up in flames."
Lev drew a big smile on their rock
friend's face with some cool ashes.

The sun was slowly setting.
Lev and Levi leaned back against
the belly of their rocky friend.
"Maybe now we know all there is to know."

They were tired but happy.
They looked out over the water,
where one seagull had found the other.

But after a while, Levi shifted
this way and that. He rubbed his back.
"What's the matter?" asked Lev.
"Aren't you comfortable?"
"Not really," said Levi.
"These rocks are pretty cold and hard."

Lev agreed, moving his neck
from side to side. "I think you may be right.
He may be strong,
but he doesn't have a warm heart."

They rested there together in silence.
"I'm happy that we don't know everything
there is to know yet," Levi said at last.
"It means we can try again tomorrow."

Lev enjoyed the sunset
from the front steps.
Levi, who only this morning
had been a dot on the horizon,
sat next to him.

"Look over there," said Levi.
"The yellow butterflies are back.
They must like it here." Lev smiled.

"We've had crashing waves,
thunder and lightning, wind, and rain!"
"And we still had a great time," Levi said.
"A brilliant time, even."

The two butterflies were dancing
cheerfully around each other in the warm,
red glow of the setting sun.

Lev and Levi sat side by side in silence.
Sometimes you don't have to say anything
to be able to hear everything.

"What a stunning sunset,"
Levi said finally.
"Look how beautiful and fiery."

"Yes," Lev nodded,
"and how spectacular."

Together: A Tale of Friendship

By Daphne Decker
Illustrated by Joey Holthaus

U.S. Edition Publisher & Creative Director
Ilona Oppenheim

U.S. Edition Art Director
Jefferson Quintana

U.S. Edition Editorial Director
Lisa McGuinness

U.S. Edition Editorial Coordinator
Jessica Faroy

Printed and bound in China by Shenzhen Reliance Printers.

Together: A Tale of Friendship was first published
in the United States by Tra Publishing in 2024.

Originally published under the title *Vrienden maken* in 2023
by Fontaine Uitgevers, Amsterdam, The Netherlands.

ISBN: 978-1-962098-09-0

Tra Publishing
245 NE 37th Street
Miami, FL 33137
trapublishing.com

T tra.publishing